what women don't want to hear

written by ren marie

ISBN: 9798854165693

©
Copyright 2023

Introduction;

If, like myself, you've found yourself questioning *what do women really not want to hear,* then you're in the right place. Over the years of listening to such ballshit from fellow peers, strangers and entitled asshats, I finally decided, enough is enough. No longer will I listen to egotistical brats who I owe absolutely nowt to, nor will I continue to ignore the snarky remarks from strangers about my lifestyle choices - *I am done with hearing shite I don't need to hear about.*

So, I've written every shite remark I've heard and the reason why I'm not going to listen to it.

If you're a sensitive soul, this book definitely isn't for you. I'm a commoner with no filter, my facial expressions share my thought process and my tongue gives more back lashes then it receives.

This is the uncovered, hated, opinionated, truth of a woman living in a male dominated world.

a small note; I love men. I just don't love the twats that ruin male reputation.

any names mentioned in this book have no relation to people in real life

*This is for the old me, the people pleaser -
Times change and my heart is no longer the soft tissue it once was.*

Changing the way I thought meant my heart no longer felt like a burden.

are you ready?

No.1

"You should smile more."

Why? Who do I owe my smile to? Oh, that's right Thomas from WindiDicks, absolutely no one.
Why the fuck do I want to smile just so you can feel a little more egotistical about yourself?
No, I shouldn't smile more. You should simply fuck off more. You silly fuck.

Maybe my days been shite and all I want is to punch someone's toothy grin in, I mean, I could smile while doing it.
If you're offering, I can show you how wide I can smile.

No.2

"You'll regret not having children!"

Listen Susan, I know your home life is probably shite because your husband Dave doesn't want to deal with your exhausted mood swings and his little dick doesn't feel the same anymore but that doesn't mean you get to dictate what I will and will not regret.
I'll also regret not having time for myself, being able to drop every responsibility and say fuck it, I'm going to start a porno without having to think twice about how it's going to effect my future childrens' future.

No.3

"You should wear something tighter, and put on some make-up, you'll be more attractive that way."

Excuse me Michael, your dick is showing through your under armour boxers. Believe me, you wearing overly tight underwear does not make your cock look bigger. I can smell your month old cheese from a ten mile radius.

Listen, I know you feel the need to change someone else's appearance to feel better about your own, but, honestly, it just makes you look all that more pathetic.

and unattractive.

No. 4

"You shouldn't talk like that, it's not lady-like."

Yes, Paddy from the IT floor, I should only speak in a soft tone and only speak when spoken too.
Fuck off you silly shite.
I was born with a mouth and a brain that learnt how to speak. Infant me didn't spend months and years copying my mothers lip movements nor did the child me spend hours in school learning English just to be told I should probably stay a little more quiet and polite.

I have a mouth, a voice box, a brain
- and believe me, my brain cells are most probably wider than your manhood is.

You jealous tit.

No.5

"Women shouldn't work. You should stay at home and serve your man, treat him with respect!"

…

Pfft. I'm going to piss myself with laughter.
I refuse to be a slave to anyone, unless it's a sexual thing -
in which case, bite me bitch.

Men who say this, in my experience, are afraid because
they know once a women has a job, an income,
they're no longer needed.
They are no longer the man of the home.
Their status no longer holds any importance.

Poor buggers, welcome to a smidge of womanhood.

No.6

"You shouldn't sit with your legs open, you look like a man."

*Look, I'll be honest, like many other women who don't have an itty bitty vagina that fits nicely behind a piece of string, I physically can't keep my legs crossed/closed.
Plus, have you tried sitting like a 'woman'? That shit is uncomfortable!*

*My fanny needs air.
My comfort comes before your opinion.*

I'd rather fanny fart myself raw then do what you want me to do.

And no, I'm not going to have surgery or lose weight, I'm going to sit down, lean back and spread my legs like butter on a gram cracker.

No.7

"Women should wear lingerie for their man."

And the man should pay for it, pay for the waxing sessions I'm going to need beforehand, pay for the therapy sessions from the countless looks in the mirror doubting if we're sexy enough to please you, and also put on an outfit yourselves.

Look, woman to man here, you guys don't look all that when naked either, we want more.
Dress up, tidy up, and maybe shut the fuck up.

I like my man wearing leather straps, a silver buckled belt to whip the hell out of my back, and maybe a gimp mask for that extra bit of jumpscare.

Point is, YOU need to make an effort too. A sexy outfit is a turn on for you, same for us women.

PUT. IN. THE. SAME. EFFORT.
Wetness guaranteed.

No.8

"Is it that time of the month?"

Gerald, listen, I will single handedly rip apart every blood cell you have in that fragile body of yours and wear your teeth as a necklace and use your skin to wipe the blood coming from my vagina if you ask me that cunting question again.

There is nothing more infuriating than being asked that question, regardless if it is that time of the month or not.

If I wanted you to know when my time of the month is, I will make it obvious and paint my face with the blood clots.

Stop using our reason for our frustration on a menstrual cycle. You've probably just pissed us off by not listening.

No.9

"Stop acting like a bitch."

Jokes on you. A bitch is a dog, a dog barks, bark is on a tree, trees are nature and nature is beautiful.

Thanks for the compliment.

..

Jokes aside, just shut the fuck up.
The next male that calls me a bitch as an insult I'm going to personally show you why size matters.

No.10

"I can't believe you've slept with that many people, you're such a whore."

Ah, yes long legs Jimmy, I am such a whore for enjoying something.
No, what you don't like is that I've had to go through so many males because not one of them knew where my clit is or knew that pleasure was a 2 way thing.

You're afraid you'll be another almost in my pleasure diary.

No.11

"You should hurry and get married, men want young, fun women, not old hags."

Truthfully, I've always wanted that type of love that could last through the stars and time. But, I won't settle for someone who would leave over ageing.
People change.
Looks change.
Hearts change.
If you're not accepting of that, then love just isn't for you.

No.12

"Men don't like women who-"

And I give a shit, why exactly?
Look, I couldn't give two cahoots about what someone else likes or doesn't like, I am me, and that's that.
I was once a woman who would change her entirety for a man, and I learned over the years that no matter how much you change yourself for someone else, your worth to them will never change.

And I'll be truthful here, the next person, man or woman, old or young, tells me I should change this or that for a male interest, will receive my dentistry work and I shall fill your fillings with my ovaries instead.

Chew, you mutt.

No.13

"A woman should ALWAYS cook, clean and bear children for her man."

Am I your fucking mother? Are you a child?

Listen, you came from a vagina. You lived inside a woman for 9 months, it was a WOMAN who gave you shelter, nutrients, sacrificed HER body for YOU to have life.

We don't owe you shit.

You owe us your life.
You owe just as we owed.

Women should not do shite to please a man's needs UNLESS they personally want too.

And if we decide to carry your legacy inside our bodies for 9 months and then take care of said legacy, you best be grateful because when a woman has a child, their entire thought process changes. We realise our worth through our children.
We realise the difference between true love and fake love.

No.14

"Women belong in the kitchen. Make me a sandwich."

Richard, look, your brain cells are falling out of that big'ol mouth of yours. The fact that some men believe this is what gets me.

Men will go through life without learning how to feed themselves, relying on women to cook for them but then will slate the women for cooking something not quite to their taste.

I have some advice for those men;
Starve.

No.15

"Are you a virgin?"

That matters, why?
Surely this shouldn't matter as much as it does.
I know men like the feeling of 'deflowering' a woman, but, when it boils down to it, this is actually quite creepy.
Men like that control of being the one to take away a woman's innocence, this, by the way, shows the red flag of possession.

They seem to think deflowering a woman gives them the right of ownership.

News flash to all men here; 9 times out of 10, any slightly round and long object we find in a desperate horny state was what we really lost our virginity too. Not your dick.
Sorry.

No.16

"...but, you're a girl."

Correction, I'm a woman. And you're an egotistical turd with a snail brain.

My gender shouldn't define what I'm capable of. I can understand strength, and a few other things due to the scientific difference between a male and female anatomy, but there are many things a female can do that a man can also do.

No.17

"You should shave, women shouldn't have hair."

*No Billy, women should have hair. You just have a preference for women without it.
Just like I have a preference for big dicks without a male attached.*

*Plus, you can't say shit when I can grow more body hair then you can.
p.s my moustache is better than yours.*

No.18

"When are you going to have another baby?"

I was asked this less than a week after having my first baby. A WEEK.
7 fucking days Karen.
I was so adamant I was 1 and done.
I still have haemorrhoids swelling my asshole up and my poor fanny feels like a beetroot - and to top it off, my stomach ended up being cut open in an emergency caesarean. All I thought about is how much my first postpartum shit is going to absolutely obliterate my entire body.

I didn't even know what day it was. My biggest concern was making sure my son was fed and looked after, Not when am I going to rent my uterus for another 9 months.

Heads up, 3 months pp and I totally want another baby. Despite being adamant I was 1 and done.

Fuck you Karen for being right.

No.19

"Is your outfit appropriate for your age?"

Look, I can understand if I was wearing lingerie outside, but if I want to wear a noot noot Pingu top or go on a full on emo outfit, I'm going to do so regardless of my age. Let me live in my emo phase for a little while longer, I haven't reached my thirties yet.

No.20

"You're a lady, you shouldn't have tattoos or piercings!"

Oh Judith, will you shove off? Yes, I get it, back in your day you had to be prim and proper and it was hella frowned upon to be anything but angelic looking, Times have changed, punks' returning in full swing and I love being covered in reckless ink and slightly wonky piercings that were done in high school bathrooms.
Yes, I admit, I do look a little robust and scary, but, that's a good thing! I hate people anyway, so it benefits me.
I don't give a shit about you.

Nor does my cat tattoos and prison barcode looking K924 across my neck. Which, FYI, it's not from prison. It's my cat's spay number - yes, I know.

No.21

"You shouldn't eat that."

*Listen Fiona, we can't all look like an ogre one minute then a princess the next regardless of what we eat.
I know I shouldn't eat that, some people shouldn't own guns, have kids and/or animals, or even be alive!
Unfortunately your opinion is much like what comes out of my ass after a silly amount of dairy
- unimportant, painful, and forgotten about when I see my father in laws mac'n'cheese.*

No.22

"You should follow in the footsteps of your sibling."

Oh, this ol'chestnut. The amount of times I've been told I should be the exact carbon copy of my sister, funny thing is, she now absolutely despises my existence for no other reason other than plain jealousy and being so up her own backside she forgot how close we used to be.
Money oriented bitch.

The more you tell a child or an adult this, and then the more they try to please this idea of yours, the more they forget who they are.
Pretending to be someone else for others benefits and wants, ends up with you alone, losing yourself and having to figure it all out over and over again.
And believe me, sometimes remembering the person you once were, is more painful than losing yourself.

No.23

"You should forgive and forget!"

No I bloody well should not.
Forgiveness and forgetting may be good for some people, but not for everyone. I personally want to remember why I despise someone so much that the memory shakes me to my core each time I look at them and my inner serial killer lurks its way to the surface.

I'm petty, yes, but I'm not a pushover.
Not anymore.

No.24

"But they're your family! You shouldn't cut them off."

*Being blood related does not give you a get-out-of-jail pass. Nor is it reason enough to treat me like shit.
I'll give you a couple examples, mentioning the one above;
Now, I loved my sister, but her ignorance and money oriented and top dog nature has ruined whatever sisterly bond we had. She always needed to be the best, at everything, and I surpassed her, and boy, does she not like that. Now, she's ignored me for 2 years, without giving me a reason, is adamant on telling everyone that my rapist and abuser is a nice man and that I'm drama, anything to make her seem better (she also was obsessed with my ex husband, the abuser, thinking he liked her more than me) - the day she crawls back, will be the day of bliss. And even if she doesn't, I don't need that kind of patheticness lacing my good vibes.*

*Another example, my darling elderly nana, asked me to have my first pregnancy, first miscarriage, at my mothers home so while I bled out my daughter, I could look after the pets while she gallivanted on holiday.
Then called me selfish when I said no due to my current situation.*

So yes, I can cut any fucker off.

No.25

"The man should provide for his family!"

This one really fucks me off. Why the hell do I have to rely on a man to take care of me and any offspring I produce? I can do that. I can be a mother, employee, first aider, chef, nanny - I can be everything at once and still find time for myself.

I'm going to be blunt here, I'd much rather be sweating my non-existent balls off every day earning my own money and securing my own future, then rely on someone who when and if they decide to leave for someone else means I'm completely fucked and lose everything.
No, fuck that.

If I want something, it's my responsibility to get it, at any means possible.

No.26

"You should get that mummy makeover, bit of lipo, flab removal…"

Look, Barbie, I ain't about that plastic shite.
Yes, my stomach currently overhangs and I can't even see my vagina at this point but I don't need to get shit.
My body is a fucking life giver, a temple, a beautiful reminder at how grateful I should be for having carried my wonderful children.
I don't need your crappy opinions about how I should change my body and go under the knife to suit society's beauty standards.

I would much rather sit back, eat a damn cupcake, use my extra rolls as a cushion for my children to lay on and hold my middle finger up to every cunt that thinks otherwise. When I feel the want to change myself, it'll be on my terms. Not yours.

No.27

"You should cover up your postpartum body. No one wants to see those stretch marks."

My hell, the amount of times throughout my pregnancy I was told how I should use bio oil, different creams etc to reduce or get rid of my growing stretch marks that cover 75% of my stomach.

They tell you to have children, then tell you how disgusting and ruined you are afterwards.
It's like sex, they help you undress, but never help you get dressed.

My body is my body, my body grew a child, stretched, hurt, held life. And I'll be damned if an 87 year old gremlin tried to dictate to me about something that's not of their concern.

In other words, bugger off you old goose.

No.28

"Women shouldn't have short hair."

Gary, men shouldn't have a mouth to talk from if that's the type of shite that comes out of it.
It's up to the woman, it's their belonging, you have no right to say what she should or shouldn't do with her own body, hair, blah blah blah.

Look, if you don't have something major to offer, we're not going to bat an eye at your opinions.
Your receding hairline is no match for us, period.

No.29

"You're asking for it."

Oh yes, Peter, I asked for your opinions, lustful stare at my tits and overall disgusting experience because I greeted you back in a friendly manner so I wouldn't get your usual snobby, sarcastic, mouth breather attitude with a lecture on how and why ignoring your greeting is a bad move.

Me wearing a low cut top, mini skirt and punk boots is me asking for your attention - no Peter, what I wear is for my own gain, my platform boots however, I wear for two reasons

1. *They're sexy as fuck*
2. *So I can smush all of my enemies under the rubber sole*

No.30

"You shouldn't drink so much alcohol, think of your future children!"

People who tell you this are just pure asshats. I don't really drink, maybe twice a year, and on those rare occasions that I do, the backlash I receive makes me cackle like the wicked witch on west street.
I'm told to think of my children, think of the example I'm making for them and my family name. News flash Terrica, I don't give a toss. I'm allowed a break from my responsibilities, from my life that I cater 24/7 for .
Sometimes, a woman just needs to let loose to simply survive.

And if you don't agree with that, then I pity the woman who goes coo coo on your ass.

No.31

"You should take his name when you get married!"

Fucking why? Why in the hell would that benefit me unless he was rich, fancy and loaded. I didn't change my name so many times to just give it up. That's part of my identity, why do I, the woman, have to give that up?
I already agreed to rent out my uterus for 9 months, why do I have to lose my name to a man that could up and leave whenever he wanted?
Do you know how much of a pain in the ass it is to change all of my identification again after a divorce?
Not only that, why would I want that reminder of being divorced?
If I hated them enough to get divorced, then bet your ass I am never taking someone else's name but my own.

Screw you old ways, I refuse to take anything but my own.

No.32

"Does your partner allow you/know you're out? How does he feel about you going out?"

JUST BECAUSE I'M IN A RELATIONSHIP OR A MARRIAGE DOES NOT MEAN THEY HAVE OWNERSHIP OF ME.
I am still my own person, I don't need permission to live a life that is rightfully mine. I will tell my partner I'm going to do something and I will listen to what they have to say about it, but the decision is ultimately up to me, not them.

*I really hate this way of thinking, **commitment is not ownership**.*

No.33

"I'm a nice guy! Why are you being like this?"

Listen Daryl, I took you out of both the friendship and relationship zone for a reason. You're not a nice man, you're a prick, plain and simple. You think because you showed a few nice compliments that I owe you my entire life and interest.
What these 'nice guys' don't realise is, 9 times out of 10, you're just plain ass creepy and vindictive.

We feel sorry for you, so we show a little care and you latch on like a newborn to their mothers nipple. And when we pull the reins in, make it so stupidly clear that friendship is all you're getting, you ignore it.
Because the truth is, friendships between women and men are secretly viewed as something more.
Yes, I contradicted myself there.

Did you notice?

We, us women, are just as bad as men.

But, don't pretend to be a 'nice guy' when you're twitching gives your anger management issues away.

No.34

"He's only tormenting you because he secretly likes you!"

Carol, fuck the fuck off you silly nightmare women. I don't care if he likes me, if the cunt says or does one more thing to fuck me off I'll take myself to jail!
Him liking me is not an excuse for him to get away with bullying behaviour!
Please, stop teaching your daughters that this is acceptable behaviour. It's a vile way to be bullied and taught that being tormented is just another way of being loved and that we should be happy about it.
Fuck that with an ounce of cocaine.
I'd rather feel the wrath of a million pitch forks than deal with a man 'liking me' and using violence as a way to show it.

I am not a fucking doll to be beaten around.

No.35

"You shouldn't stare at men like a piece of meat!"

And as Denise in P.S I love you explains it: "..and after centuries of men looking at my tits instead of my eyes, and pinching my ass instead of shaking my hand, I now have the divine right to stare at a man's backside with vulgar, cheap appreciation if I want to.".

Need I say more?

P.S. I Love You, [Film] 2007.

No.36

"Stop being so dramatic."

This just makes me want to be so much more dramatic.

No.37

"You'd be much prettier if.."

And you'd be less likely to end up in the morgue if you just learned to shut that mouth every once in a while and realise your opinions don't mean shit.

Yes, I probably would be your idea of pretty if I did numerous of different things but, why the fucking hell should I? I don't owe you shit Kevin from high school who has had no real importance to me.
You boring fart with greasy hair that somewhat resembles something from my nightmares.

Now piss off.

No.38

"It was only a compliment."

And it would be only one punch in the balls if you stare at my rack again quoting how one looks so plump.

I never understood why this was so acceptable, to be made to feel grateful to a man for complimenting my baby feeders. Yes, you think of my big'ol titties as a sexual thing, I just find it weird because I view them as milk production sacks that make me feel like a bloody cow at a slaughterhouse.

A compliment is something sweet, something nice and warm, not a lust filled intent with a side of creepy. So no, it's not just a compliment, it's a cringy asshole.

No.39

"Oh, you're one of those women."

I'm one of those women, do you mean the ones who can't be arsed to bend to your desire and will not think twice about telling you to fuck off? Then yes, if you mean that type, I'm gladly one of those women.

You just don't like that some women are learning their worth and realising we don't have to deal with your shit anymore.

You self absorbed twit.

No.40

"Always a bridesmaid, never a bride."

That's by fucking choice Marty, I don't want to deal with waking up to the same asshole for the rest of my life having to pretend that I don't want to smash his brains in with my new platform boots.

People say this like it's such a bad thing, it's a fucking blessing not having to smell the same shit stained toilet every evening when you finally want a relaxing bath.

I'd much rather attend every wedding as a bridesmaid, that way I get free booze and a shit ton of free food to stuff in my bag. And hey, if there's fish sticks, bonus treats for my cats, bitches!

No.41

"Your biological clock is ticking."

*And so is my fucking patience with your shite.
I don't care. If it runs out, great, more holidays and booze for me.
I have no idea why you seem to think my biological clock has anything to do with you, you complete munter.
I want to fuck as many people as I want, drink as much as I want, dance as much as I want, the last shit that was on my mind is when my ovaries are going to cascade out of my vagina as shriveled up mushroom looking balls.*

No.42

"You look like a woman now."

Oh, if only you could see my face while I write this. I'll give you a hint, you know how your expression shrivels up from both disgust and disbelief? Yeah, that's the one.

What a load of fucking bollocks this shit is.

I forgot what I wore, and how I tied my hair and placed my makeup defined what was in my pants.

Silly me, for thinking my DNA and anatomy was what defined my gender.

No.43

"Women just aren't funny."

I'm not even going to entertain this one. I make myself laugh, that's all I care about.

No.44

"You shouldn't gain muscles, you'll look like a man."

That's fine with me Susan, I'll be a very pretty man then. I know you're just worried that you'll end up finding me so damn attractive that poor Jeremy won't stand a chance.

I mean, I don't blame you.

I'm fucking sexy when I can be arsed to sort myself out.

At least I know where the dingaling is.

All jokes aside, I've been told this so many times. I no longer give a toss about looking like a man, I'll be strong and healthy, I'm happy and content with that.

No.45

"That's just what women are made for!"

We're not made for your entertainment. We are not made to make you feel more in power, We're not made to be submissive. We're not made to be your sexual desires for a momentary feeling. We're not made just to carry children. We're not made to look after grown adults. We're not made to be at your disposal.
We are made to be human, just as you are.
Some men seem to forget that.

No.46

"*insert catcall here*"

It's boring. It's creepy. We don't feel special, we feel repulsed. Instead of catcalling from your white vans, stop, think, reevaluate your decisions.

Catcalling does not impress women, it's tiring. Buy her some flowers instead, or a coffee, hell, give her a sweet compliment, or recite something poetic.
Not 'oioi' from your window because trust me, she will dry up and hit menopause 10 years earlier.

No.47

"I can show you a good time."

Yes, Dave69 from Wheatfield, I'm sure the 69 in your name implies exactly what you mean by 'good time'.

I'm not sure why men think women want to hear this, it's like, I might as well just give my vagina a rug burn because I'd probably get more pleasure out of that than sitting across from this sleazebag.

Get better material, it's like listening to the same scam over and over. Predictable, boring, repetitive.

No.48

"I bet I can turn you straight."

I'm not gay, but hearing that would make me delve deep into another womens down below.

Men, there is nothing to gain here, she just simply doesn't want your maggot.

Saying this doesn't make you irresistible, if anything, it makes you more repulsive.

No.49

"Your career can wait, you need to start a family."

To start a family, I need a good paying career, and no, the man will not be the provider. This is already a male dominated world, why give the men more financial power?

No.50

"You women never know what you want!"

We do, you just don't like the answer we give you so you ignore it and pretend as if we're still deciding on a response.

Immaturity at its finest.

You throw your toys out of the pram, but still, will expect the woman to tidy up after you.

You don't get it, do you? Women are more mature, we know what we want and what we need, we just get told to shut up, sit up and tidy up.

Absolute horse shit.

No.51

"You've been so full of yourself since having a baby."

It's funny how many times I've been told this, and my answer stays the same.
Yes, I am full of myself. I am full from exhaustion, hormonal changes, postpartum hair loss, being dictated to, being told how I should and shouldn't parent my child, being told to ask for help if I need it but then when I do it's such a chore for the other person, not fitting in my pregnancy clothes despite losing the baby weight.
I am full of myself because I've learnt just how real stranger danger is, just how real new mother fear can rip you limb from limb.
I am full of myself because I just want my baby to stay safe.
So excuse me if I tell you to back the fuck away from my child.

No.52

"Are you really not going to do that for me?"

I am not your fucking mother.
You are not a child.
You are an adult.
Get the fuck up you silly twit.

I hate this. Just because I am a mother, does not mean I have to baby a fully grown ass man.
If you don't know how to cook; learn or starve.
If you can't be arsed to clean up after yourself; get the fuck out of my apartment.
If you don't want to sort your own life out and think I should fix it for you; news flash ya little cunt, I ain't going to do shit for you.

Grow the fuck up and stop relying on women to fix and baby you.

No.53

"She's crazy."

*Yes, George, I'm crazy because your incompetence and lazy attitude finally drove me to that point.
Men, do you not understand that women do not switch off? We can't, there is so much we have to take responsibility for that we never even asked to have to begin with. It just came with being a woman!*

Who the hell do you think cleans up the clothes you throw around the place? The food in the fridge? The casserole sitting on top of the oven? Clean, pristine floors? No dust? No bad smell? Fresh washing? No dirt in the bathtub or stains around the toilet?

It's not the fucking tooth fairy that's for sure!

Women did not ask for this role, we were told we had to do this. Regardless of whether we wanted to or not, we are told to start a family, forget our career choice, clean up, tidy up, maintain your figure, have and raise 3 or 4 children.

*While you work, we move mountains.
But yes Dick, you work 8 hours a day.
Try 24/7.*

No.54

"But, I've been looking after them for hours now!"

They're your fucking children, of course you should be taking care of them. It's a full time fucking job!

*This really grinds my fanny into pure dryness.
Men, understand this, we need a breather too.
We need our own time, and I don't mean a 20 minute bath with the door wide open. I mean a day. Maybe even the weekend.*

No.55

"I'm so glad you look like your pictures."

Yes, but why do you look like the father version of yours, 25 year old Donnie who looks 47.

No.56

"You're a woman, you should know how to…"

Let me guess Steve from HR that sits behind his desk, I should know how to clean, cook, look after children, myself, maintain an entire army while you sit there for 8 hours tapping away.
It's not that I should know, you inconsiderate prick, it's that I have no other choice but to know about this.
This wasn't a taught thing, this was a pushed-on-us-from-a-young-age thing.
This was a give-the-girls-baby-dolls so they learn how to mother them from a young and impressionable age.

This is a ballshit way of forcing women from a young age to bend to society's wants.
So fuck you Steve from HR.

No.57

"You're quite smart, you know, for a woman."

Oh damn, I never knew having a vagina made me naturally dumb.

I have a point to this actually - go to the next one

No.58

"Dumb blonde."

*Why does hair colour equate to the level of a persons' IQ?
Oh that's right, because a lot of male written movies created this stereotype.*

*It's such a ballache stereotype.
I could have a mother fucking rainbow on my head and I'd still be as smart as I am now.*

If men actually think this is true, then I think we need to create a new stereotype; if you have a cock, you have a small cock.

Yeah, now that's a dumb blonde.

No.59

"You should use all of these anti ageing products, skin products, body scrubs. Use aloe vera, you can't have razor bumps! You need to stay looking young and fresh."

I'm sorry
When did I start giving a shit about what you fucking want?
Most of the products give you thrush, rashes, burns - have you ever used hair removal cream? No? Imagine a fresh razor cut and shove mint tea tree shower gel on it.
Did you cringe?
Welcome to womanly products.

Don't tell us what to fucking do when you still have dingle berries attached to your arse hair!

No.60

"You'll never survive without men."

Correction, no one would survive without semen or a womb and all the insides. We can however, survive without the attitude that comes with a man.
We have strap ons and dildos for a reason.

Thank fucccccck.

No.61

"Awh, are your panties in a twist?"

Derek, the funny part of this is my frustration brought more pleasure to my panties then your lil maggot ever did.

This is such an annoying question. And to be quite blunt here, I will not hesitate to punch and step on your maggot if you ask me that fucking question again.

It's a taunting, gaslighting, pisstake question and they know it'll piss us off more, so, I'm going to react in an unlady-like manner and pelt my fist into their goonies with a smile.

Yes, now I will 'smile more'.

No.62

"Get over it."

I will twist your nipple so hard and fold your cock up like a tea towel if you tell me one more time to get over something that's bothering me.
As a woman, we are expected to just get over any trauma that has any remote attachment to men. Why? Because the fuckers can't accept the responsibility.

Typical, but it'll be the woman's fault.

No.63

"You're overreacting"

Says the 'man' that'll throw a hissy fit because he was asked to get off his game and pay attention to his child. But yes, you dick face turd arse looking mother fucker, I'm the one who is overreacting.

Or is it because you've driven me to my absolute fucking limit with countless begging you to get up and help me that I finally had enough of your shite and gave you an explosion of well deserved anger?

Fucking pure a-hole.

No.64

"Well, you owe me this. I did this thing for you 5 years ago so you still owe me."

You looked after my pet for 2 hours while I went to work, but yes despite the countless thanks I gave you, cooking you food, cleaning your clothes etc - I still owe you.

Fuck off Jimmy.

I don't owe shit, and I hate how you still feel like I owe you when we all know, women do SO much more for their partners, family, home - shit, even the animals of the household get fed before we do.

No.65

"You owe me a thank you. I did your job!"

Yes, Brett, my job. My job is apparently picking up your cum stained rags from under the bed and putting them in the wash, making your dinners, your appointments, washing up every cutlery, plate, bowl and hell only knows what else because you can't be arsed to do it yourself. My job is staying up until 3am each night cleaning our home so it's at least sanitary for your bigfooted cunt arse. Yes this is my job. And I should so totally bow down and worship you because you did the most human thing and picked up your own cum stained rags. Granted you moved them a foot away from the bed and not in the wash, but yes, well done you.

No.66

"Women are so high maintenance."

Asking for help is high maintenance nowadays.

The reality is, we're not high maintenance, we're just expected to have a really low standard for men and to not complain about it.

No.67

"I'll order for you."

When it comes to food, men, do not order for us. We may struggle to know where we want to eat, but not what we want to eat. And for the love of everything unholy, if you order us a fucking salad, be prepared.
We will show you how lethal pigs can be when they're hungry.

No.68

"Dyed hair/septum piercing etc is a red flag on a woman."

*Is it the rebellion against your beauty standard that you don't like? I am pretty certain that creativity in appearance does not mean crazy.
You're crazy if you think that.*

I've noticed the men who say this are usually the ones who stay in their rooms and look up porn on the daily and wear ankle supports on their wrists.

Nice try PussyBlaster6000.

No.69

"You're such a feminist."

No shit.

Anything I say that remotely supports women makes me a feminist.

So fuck it, sure.

You bald headed fuck.

No.70

"Wow, you've definitely, you'know, let yourself go a bit."

Why yes, thank you for noticing. This is what you call too-busy-to-look-after-myself-because-I'm-currently-babying-an-adult-mama's-boy.
As you can see Carol, I was given priorities, and myself definitely wasn't one of them.
But my hell, if I prioritised myself over the 'man of the house' I would no longer have any status to stand on let alone survive on.

No.71

"Women should only speak when spoken to."

And you should shut up before I ram this reason down your throat.
Put it this way, I am not your property, you don't own me so therefore, you have no say whatsoever in what I do and do not do.

To put this in simple, gamer terms

Alt F4 and fuck off.

No.72

"You're not like other girls."

No Jeremy, because I am a woman.
Calling me a girl just makes me cringe and think you have skeletons in your closet that need to be addressed by a therapist.

No.73

"You're too emotional."

This one, I need to explain. Because, this isn't a man's fault. This is learnt behaviour from former generations. Men have been taught that showing emotions is a sign of weakness, so, when a woman can openly show how they feel, even if it's a miniscule amount, men can't register or understand it so they're natural instinct/reaction to this is anger.

Hopefully, this can be fixed. Fixed as in, men find that safety net where they can show emotion and undo former generations teachings.

*So for the men on this one, I stand with you.
But, I will still get pissed about it.*

No.74

"You're a woman. It's natural for you to love babies and want some of your own."

No, it really fucking isn't. A lot of women hate the idea of having children, hate the idea of becoming relied on, having to rethink every choice they make, losing their independence - it's not natural, what is natural is being tired of hearing the same shit and being expected to just go along with it because she has a fucking womb.

No.75

"Women don't like to use curse words."

Can you believe this fucking shite?

Hahahahahahahahahahahahahahahahahahahahahaha hahahahahahahahahahahahahahahahahahahahahahah ahahahahahahahahahahahahahahahahahahahahahaha hahahahaha!

You fucking doughnut.

No.76

"Women don't know how to use tools, so they need a man to do it."

Question for ya:
Have you ever seen a determined woman hang up a photo frame?
We don't need levellers, tape measures, hammers etc. All we need is eyesight, an arm and the back of a shoe or the TV remote.

Job done.

When we ask you, it's to make you feel better about yourself.

No.77

"You haven't had a real man."

I don't fucking want one.

No.78

"Women only like romance comedies."

Ok, yes, I do love my romance 2000's movies. I can't help it. But I also love Kdramas, horrors, documentaries, anime, cartoons -
Point is, we like more than what we're given credit for.
So stick on a 1945 horror and crack on.

No.79

"Women only wear matching lingerie to get laid."

*I wear my granny pants to get laid.
I buy matching sets, very rarely, because, at times, I feel good and want to feel sexy. Not for my mans' approval, I dress up for my own approval.*

Honestly, if my man doesn't have leather gear on, a gimp mask, leather whip with spiked balls on the end or hell, a Wartenburg pinwheel then I don't want it nor am I wearing anything other than my granny pants.

No.80

"Women don't watch porn! That's for the men."

We watch it, sometimes on the regular.

But most of us don't watch straight porn.
Most of us straight women like lesbian porn.
Because truthfully, men suck so bad in porn.

'You like that baby?' Oh yes, wow, thank you. Noiceee.

No.81

"Every woman loves to shop for clothing, handbags and shoes."

I don't know about you, but I fucking hate physical shopping. Trying on clothes in stores, doing what almost feels like the walk of shame when you have to give it back to the store clerk knowing that the outfit you were so excited about, was too small despite being the same size for years - yeah, no thank you.
Shopping is not relaxing, it is the most stressful, body shattering thing known to women.

Plus, to the commoner folk, these prices nowadays, I'd rather spend jail time.

No.82

"Women can't like beer, that's a man's drink!"

Then call me a fucking man because I love that shit.

Wine is absolute shite and smells like fucking nail polish remover.
Only incredibly posh totties drink that and can stand it for their image.

No.83

"You look really tired today."

Yeah, I'm tired of your shit Susan.
Instead of reminding me how tired I look, maybe just shut the fuck up?

No.84

"Wow! You look so much better now that you've lost all that weight."

And my popularity grew, secret admirers became more existent, I wasn't ignored, brushed off or treated like shit. It's funny how quickly everyone forgets the person you are just because your appearance changed.

*I'm still me.
And this shit still hurts.*

No.85

"Listen."

No.

You shit stick.

No.86

"I bet you taste good."

The fuck.
No.
Fuck off you grim reaper shit fuck.

Yes, I do taste good but that's not for you.
Anyone else find this fucking creepy as hell?
And then they say how they want to taste your juices…

You should taste holy water, but even then I don't think that'll help you.

No.87

"You should be grateful you have big tatas."

I am.
They're great.
Bouncy.

But my fucking scoliosis spine hurts quite a fucking bit. I'd like to lie down without being suffocated. Run without being knocked out. Put on a loose shirt without looking 8 months pregnant from how far my tatas have pushed the material out.

I love my big tatas, but I'm also not grateful for them. When I speak in a room full, they're part of the attention. Getting what I want? I got it. Not because of my IQ, but because they're the main attraction at an interview.
Or, women you know this, the death stare from the itty titty community.

It's not my fault you have sardines and I have fucking beluga whales.

No.88

"You have a pretty mouth, it'll look even better wrapped around my cock."

Oh the road to cannibalism is becoming more and more realistic.

Listen, I don't want to be anywhere near your cheese smelling rotten cock. Go and have a bleach bath.
You stink.

Seriously, do they think this is attractive?

No.89

insert cringy compliment from man.
We don't react
"Well you're just a fucking slag anyway, whore."

How does that resort to pure anger?
Why the fuck would I even want to answer your mangy arse when your true colours show soon after?

Men, please, sort your fucking selves out.
If your compliment is a sexual one, high chance if you're not our partner, you're making us uncomfortable and because we don't feel comfortable enough to respond, instead of just taking it on the chin, you fuckers prove to us why we shouldn't ever respond.

But some of you, believe we owe you that response. And to those men that believe that shit-

go fuck yourself.

No.90

"Women should only wear petite jewellery, not thick chains or watches."

I used to wear an ex's of mines' watch. It was a bulky, military type watch. I loved it. I loved the thickness on my slim wrist, I loved feeling the heaviness of that watch and how it made me feel somewhat equal to a man, even for a split second.

So, Jeremy, if I want to fucking wear a bulky piece of jewellery, I'm going to fucking do so.

Especially if I'm the one paying for the cunting thick piece of bling.

You're just jealous your charity shop wedding band has faded so badly that it's camouflaged into your skin.

You fucking mongtrot.

No.91

"You're such a tease."

Yes, Terry17463 from Somerset, still living in his mothers' basement at the ripe age of 45, me responding to your advances with a monotone attitude and blunt 'I'm not interested.' is me being a tease.

Some of you men really make me want to use a sledge hammer on my own clit.

No.92

"You're so frigid."

I'm not frigid, it's just that your cock is not worth my vaginal time.

I've always hated that word, frigid. I was called frigid when I was 15/16 years old. Still a kid. A fucking kid.
The most hilarious part? It was an adult who called me frigid.

You twisted fuck.

No.93

"You can't do *insert job here*! You're too small and cute looking."

Do they think this is a mother fucking compliment? Stop telling me what I can and can't do. My appearance shouldn't affect my capability of being able to do something.
You fucking bigot fucking arse wipe.

This isn't, ya'know, something we want to hear. This is just an asshole move.

You just come across as an absolute prick.

No.94

"Fathers should get praised for doing the bare minimum."

Where's my fucking 'well done you'?
Why is it, that cunting Gregory, will get a pat on the back and 20 different praises for doing something as simple as taking his children to the shop!
But, oh, if a mum takes her child to the shop - we get zilch. No smiles from strangers, just judgemental stares for taking a 6 year old to the grocery store during school hours.

I love how a father will get so much acknowledgement for the simplest of things, but a mother, it's expected of us so no need for a well done on our end.

What a load of croc shit.

We want a 'well done' every now and again!

No.95

"How are you still single?"

Because you're a twat.
And I don't settle for less than I deserve.

No.96

"Wow, I forget that women know absolutely everything."

Yes, Rob, we fucking do and not by interest and choice either. We have to learn this shit because some men expect this or are too lazy to actually learn about life and it's left up to the woman to sort your shit out!

And if we don't do this shit for you, you bet your ass we know you'll spread so much shit that jail looks like a vacay for us.
You fucking idiotic pain in the arse.

No.97

"It was just a joke!"

No, a joke is something funny.
You were laughing at my expense for no reason other than you gaining some type of twisted control.
I understand you have to feel like you're the one in charge otherwise you crumble, but, if you make one more fucking joke at my expense and I will quite literally rip your cunting balls off and shove them in you eye sockets and guess where your eyes would be going?

You'll be seeing with clouded eyes, you sweaty fucker.

No.98

"All you women do is complain!"

Or maybe if you got of your lazy mother fucking arse, we wouldn't have shite to complain about. It's like you want us to complain and enjoy our complaining because no matter how much you acknowledge our 'complaining', you still don't fucking sort the reason why out!

I think men secretly LOVE hearing us get annoyed with their lazy side. It's like they think, oooh, extra attention. But then will call you bat shit cray cray for it.

Men, get a grip, you don't even know what you want yourselves!

No.99

"You should be happy I didn't [much worse scenario]."

Are you fucking kidding me?
I should be happy you acted the way you did, because you could have acted worse?

What in the absolute fuckery is this?

I swear the ones who say this, should be in an asylum. Preferably strapped down, castrated, with their tongue torn out.

Are you trying to force me into some twisted submission through fear and gratitude? You sick fuck.

This, I've heard before, and it still leaves me gobsmacked and angry.

Fuck you.

No.100

"Boys will be boys."

This one's my favourite.

Because

I'll show you how girls can be worse.

are you ready men?

what men don't want to hear

written by ren marie

©
Copyright 2023

a short pisstake collection for the snowflakes that'll get offended easily.

No.1

"No."

The end.

Citation list:

No.35: *P.S I love you.*[Film] LaGravenese, R. (Director), Rogers, S (Screenwriter), LaGravenese, R.(Screenwriter). 2007, Warner Bros. Pictures.

Printed in Great Britain
by Amazon